MILITARY VEHICLES

U.S. NAVY SUBMARINES

by Thomas K. Adamson

Reading Consultant:
Barbara J. Fox
Reading Specialist
North Carolina State University

Capstone press

Mankato, Minnesota

Blazers is published by Capstone Press,
151 Good Counsel Drive, P.O. Box 669, Mankato, Minnesota 56002.
www.capstonepub.com

Books published by Capstone Press are manufactured with paper
containing at least 10 percent post-consumer waste.

Library of Congress Cataloging-in-Publication Data
Adamson, Thomas K., 1970–
    U.S. Navy submarines / by Thomas K. Adamson.
    p. cm.—(Blazers. Military vehicles)
    Summary: "Provides an overview of the design, uses, weapons,
and equipment of U.S. Navy submarines"—Provided by publisher.
    Includes bibliographical references and index.
    ISBN-13: 978-0-7368-5471-9 (hardcover)
    ISBN-10: 0-7368-5471-1 (hardcover)
    1. Submarines—United States—Juvenile literature. 2. United
States. Navy—Juvenile literature. I. Title. II. Title: United States Navy
submarines. III. Series.
V858.A725 2006
359.9'3834'0973—dc22   2005024844

Editorial Credits
Carrie A. Braulick, editor; Thomas Emery, designer; Jo Miller, photo
    researcher/photo editor

Photo Credits
Corbis/Steve Kaufman, 5
Courtesy of the Smithsonian Institution, NMAH/Transportation, 22–23
DVIC, 17 (middle, bottom); OS2 John Bouvia, 6–7; PH1 Chris Desmond,
    20; PH1 Robert McRoy, 17 (top); PH2 August Sigur, 18; PH2 David
    C. Duncan, 13 (bottom); PH3 Michael Barth, 13 (top)
Getty Images Inc./Time Life Pictures/U.S. Navy, 9
Photo by Ted Carlson/Fotodynamics, 28–29
Photo courtesy Naval Sea Systems Command, 19
U.S. DOD graphic by Ron Stern, 15
U.S. Navy Photo, cover; Paul Farley, 27; PH1 David A. Levy, 25;
    PH3 Danielle M. Sosa, 11

Printed in the United States of America in Stevens Point, Wisconsin.
122010   006019R

TABLE OF CONTENTS

U.S. NAVY SUBMARINES

U.S. Navy submarines go where no other military vehicles can. Subs lurk quietly under the sea. At any time, they are ready to attack.

For an enemy, staying safe from a Navy sub is hard. Navy subs creep up to coasts to blast away land targets. They also rip enemy ships to shreds.

At 453 feet (138 meters) long, the USS *Jimmy Carter* is one of the U.S. Navy's largest subs.

★ ★ ★ ★ ★ ★

DESIGN

Subs are shaped like bullets.
Their shape helps them glide
through the water.

Subs have nuclear-powered engines. The engines power a propeller, which pushes the sub through the water.

BLAZER FACT

Subs with nuclear-powered engines can run 15 years before needing more fuel. The length of a sub's mission is limited only by how much food it can carry for the crew.

Subs carry ballast tanks filled with air or water. Water rushes into the tanks to make the sub dive. Water is released from the tanks to make the sub rise.

DIVING

RISING

WEAPONS AND EQUIPMENT

When a Navy sub launches a torpedo, enemy ships and subs are in trouble. Even if a torpedo misses its target, it can turn around and try again.

Subs fire missiles at targets on land. Missiles burst out of tubes on top of the sub. They can hit targets 1,000 miles (1,600 kilometers) away.

MISSILE TUBES

Sailors look into periscopes to see outside the sub. New subs have viewing equipment with cameras. These devices take up less space than periscopes do.

★ ★ ★ ★ ★

PERISCOPES

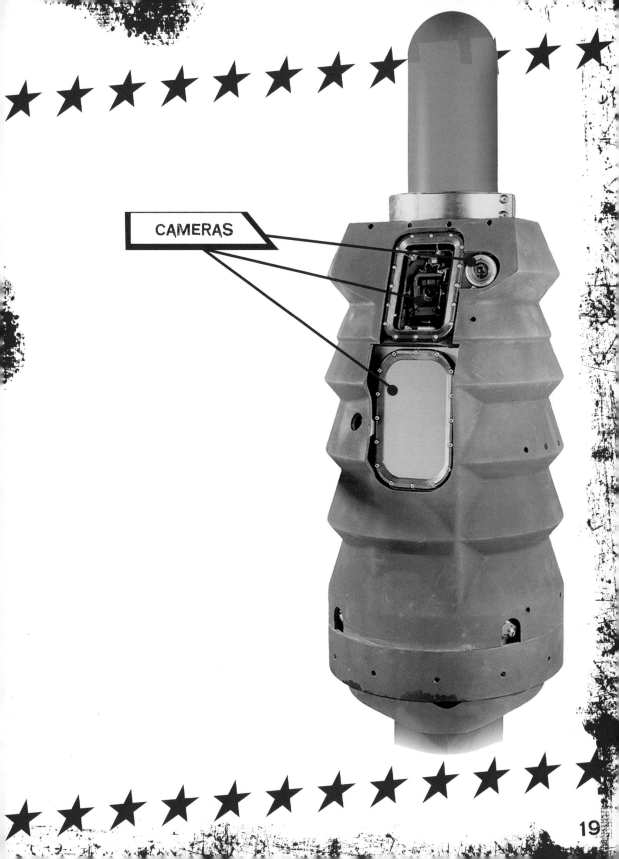

CAMERAS

19

SONAR SYSTEM

A sub's sonar system sends out sound waves that bounce off objects. The sub then locates the objects. Not even the sneakiest ship can hide from sonar.

BLAZER FACT

A sub's sonar system works like the sonar ability of bats. Bats use their sonar ability to find mosquitoes and other food.

SUB DIAGRAM

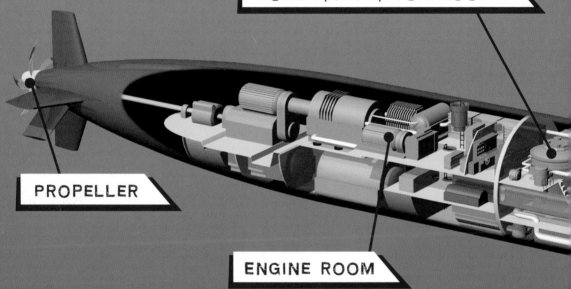

NUCLEAR REACTOR ROOM

PROPELLER

ENGINE ROOM

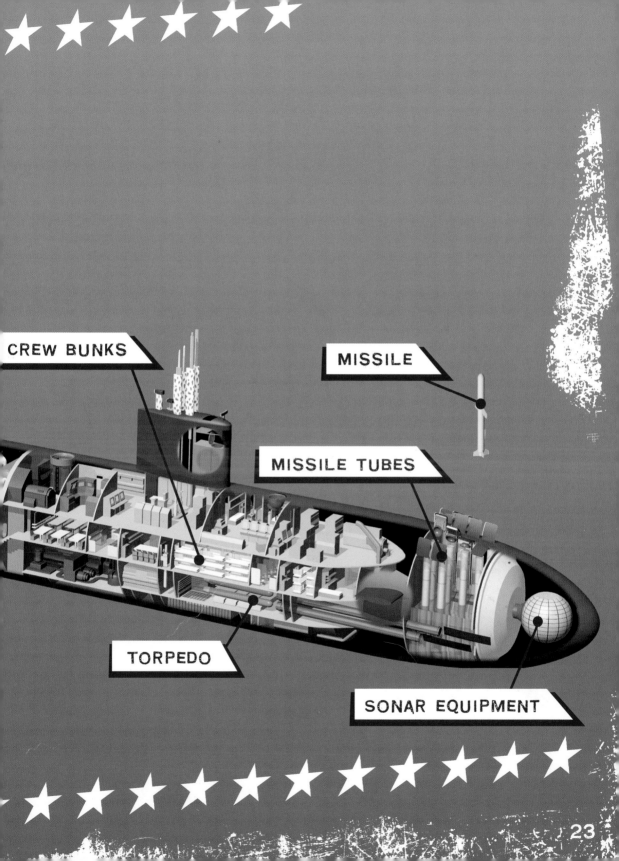

CREW BUNKS

MISSILE

MISSILE TUBES

TORPEDO

SONAR EQUIPMENT

Life on a Sub

About 140 sailors live on a sub. Some spaces are so cramped that sailors can hardly move!

Subs are at sea for months at a time. Sailors long to set foot on land. But they know their important missions help keep the United States safe.

BLAZER FACT

Subs have equipment to take salt out of ocean water. The sailors then can drink the water.

SLICING THROUGH THE SEA!

GLOSSARY

ballast tanks (BAL-uhst TANGKS)—large containers in a sub that bring in or let out water to make the sub sink or rise

coast (KOHST)—land that is next to the sea

missile (MISS-uhl)—an explosive weapon that can travel long distances

periscope (PER-uh-skope)—a tube with lenses and mirrors that allows sailors to see outside of a sub

propeller (pruh-PEL-ur)—a set of rotating blades that push a sub through water

sonar system (SOH-nar SISS-tuhm)—equipment that uses sound waves to find underwater objects

torpedo (tor-PEE-doh)—a missile that travels underwater

Read More

Baldwin, Carol, and Ron Baldwin. *U.S. Navy Fighting Vessels.* U.S. Armed Forces. Chicago: Heinemann, 2004.

Doyle, Kevin. *Submarines.* Military Hardware in Action. Minneapolis: Lerner, 2003.

Green, Michael, and Gladys Green. *Attack Submarines: The Seawolf Class.* War Machines. Mankato, Minn.: Capstone Press, 2005.

Internet Sites

FactHound offers a safe, fun way to find Internet sites related to this book. All of the sites on FactHound have been researched by our staff.

Here's how:

1. Visit *www.facthound.com*
2. Type in this special code **0736854711** for age-appropriate sites. Or enter a search word related to this book for a more general search.
3. Click on the **Fetch It** button.

FactHound will fetch the best sites for you!

INDEX